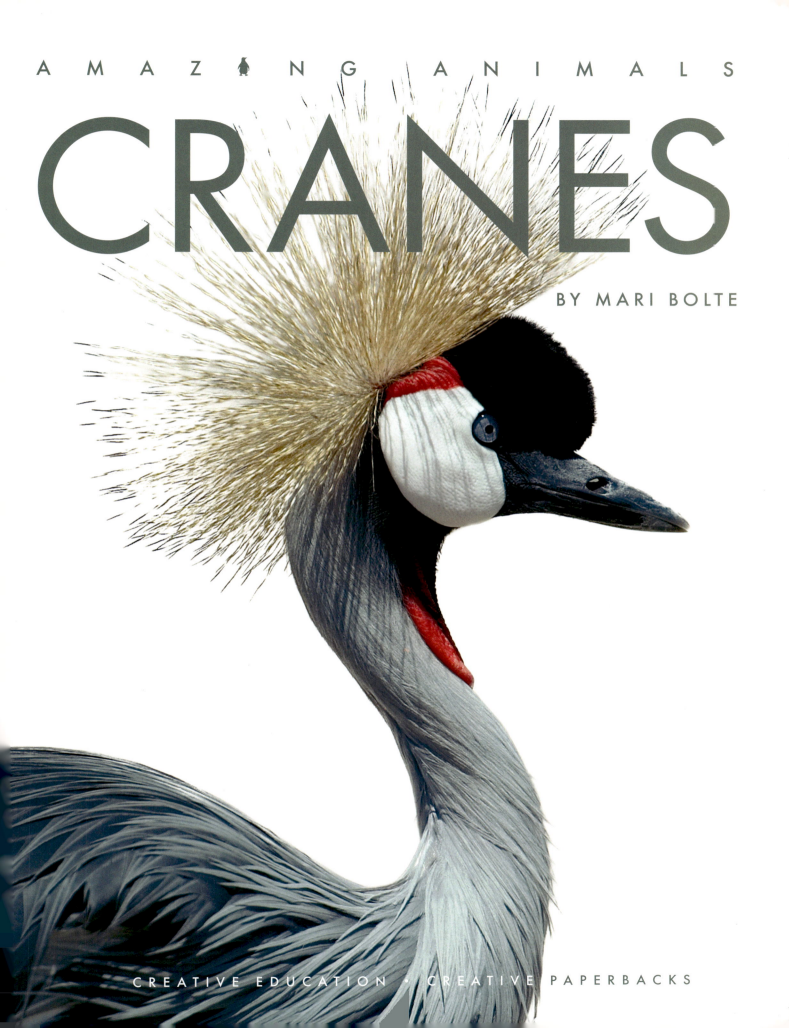

Published by Creative Education and Creative Paperbacks
P.O. Box 227, Mankato, Minnesota 56002
Creative Education and Creative Paperbacks
are imprints of The Creative Company
www.thecreativecompany.us

Design by The Design Lab
Art direction by Graham Morgan
Edited by Jill Kalz

Images by Alamy Stock Photo/James Schwabel, 8; Getty Images/Arthur Morris, 9, 17, Diane Miller, 5, scotthelfrich-photography.com, 14, Wolfgang Kaehler, 21; Pexels/A. G. Rosales, 6; Unsplash/Birger Strahl, 18, Hans Isaacson, 2, Jordi Rubies, 10, The Cleveland Museum of Art, 22–23; Wikimedia Commons/Andrea Westmoreland, 16, Leo za1, 7, Lorie Shaull, 13, Luc Viatour, cover, 1

Copyright © 2025 Creative Education, Creative Paperbacks
International copyright reserved in all countries.
No part of this book may be reproduced in any form without written permission from the publisher.

Library of Congress Cataloging-in-Publication Data
Names: Bolte, Mari, author.
Title: Cranes / by Mari Bolte.
Description: Mankato, Minnesota : Creative Education and Creative Paperbacks, [2025] | Series: Amazing animals | Includes bibliographical references and index. | Audience: Ages 6–9 | Audience: Grades 2–3 | Summary: "Discover the long-necked, long-legged crane! Explore the bird's anatomy, diet, wetland habitat, and life cycle. Captions, on-page definitions, an animal origami story, additional resources, and an index support elementary-aged kids"— Provided by publisher.
Identifiers: LCCN 2024010527 (print) | LCCN 2024010528 (ebook) | ISBN 9798889892427 (library binding) | ISBN 9781682776087 (paperback) | ISBN 9798889893530 (ebook)
Subjects: LCSH: Cranes (Birds)—Juvenile literature. | Cranes (Birds)—Behavior—Juvenile literature. | Cranes (Birds)—Life cycles—Juvenile literature.
Classification: LCC QL696.G84 B655 2025 (print) | LCC QL696.G84 (ebook) | DDC 598.3/2—dc23/eng/20240415
LC record available at https://lccn.loc.gov/2024010527
LC ebook record available at https://lccn.loc.gov/2024010528

Printed in China

Table of Contents

Look Up!	4
Find a Flock	10
Eating Everything	12
Bird Births	14
Song and Dance	18
A Crane Tale	22
Read More	24
Websites	24
Index	24

Cranes fly with their necks and legs stretched straight out.

Cranes are large, tall birds. They live everywhere except South America and Antarctica. Cranes have a long neck, a heavy bill, and a bare head. Their **plumage** is usually brown, gray, or white. There are 15 kinds of crane.

plumage feathers

Some cranes have colorful feathers on their heads.

Cranes live near marshes. Long legs help them wade through water. Cranes have four toes on their feet. Three are long and thin. They point forward. A smaller toe points backward. These toes help cranes balance in squishy mud.

marshes low wetland areas that flood during rainy seasons

A crane's body feathers overlap like shingles on a roof.

Cranes have long, soaring wings. They flap them slowly and then glide for long distances. On average, a crane's wings span 7 feet (2.1 meters). Cranes can fly up to 50 miles (80 kilometers) per hour.

span to reach from one side to another

Flocks of 20,000 cranes or more have been recorded.

Cranes like to be around other cranes. They mate for life. Families or small groups called flocks often **migrate** together. Large flocks of young birds are also common.

migrate to travel from one area to another for feeding or breeding purposes

Africa's blue cranes get their name from their feather color.

Cranes are omnivores. They hunt bugs, birds, frogs, and other small animals. They use their sharp bills to stab their food. Grass and leaves are also part of a crane's diet. So are seeds and fruit.

omnivores animals that eat both plants and animals

13

CRANES

Mated cranes build a nest on the ground with dried plants. The female usually lays two oval-shaped eggs. Both the male and the female keep the eggs warm. It takes about a month for the baby cranes to hatch.

A baby crane finds safety beneath its mother's wing.

Crane chicks are born with blue eyes and soft brown feathers. They can leave the nest just a few hours after birth. They can even swim! Chicks stay with their parents for almost a year.

Chicks can grow up to 1 inch (2.5 centimeters) per day.

Cranes are known for their dance moves. They dance to find mates and to bond with each other. Dancing cranes bob their heads. They flap their wings. They jump, bow, and toss sticks and other objects into the air.

Dancing can also be used to scare away other cranes.

Cranes are loud! They have a bugle-like call. They use it to talk to each other. Cranes also honk, purr, snore, moan, and hiss. Whooping cranes are famous for their single-note call. It can be heard for miles.

A crane call can be heard up to 2.5 miles (4 km) away.

21

CRANES

A Crane Tale

If you fold 1,000 paper cranes, your wish will come true. That's what an old Japanese story says. During World War II (1939–45), a girl named Sadako Sasaki became sick after the bombing of Hiroshima. She folded cranes and wished for a better future for everyone. People still fold cranes today to remember Sasaki and wish for peace.

Read More

Amstutz, Lisa. *Cranes*. Mankato, Minn.: Amicus, 2023.

Huddleston, Emma. *Whooping Cranes*. Minneapolis: Bearport Publishing, 2023.

Websites

Britannica Kids: Crane
https://kids.britannica.com/kids/article/crane/353010
Watch videos and learn more about cranes.

San Diego Zoo Wildlife Alliance: Crane
https://animals.sandiegozoo.org/animals/crane
Discover fun facts about crane feathers, flight, and more.

Note: Every effort has been made to ensure that the websites listed above are suitable for children, that they have educational value, and that they contain no inappropriate material. However, because of the nature of the Internet, it is impossible to guarantee that these sites will remain active indefinitely or that their contents will not be altered.

Index

bills, 4, 12
chicks, 15, 16
dancing, 19
eggs, 15
feathers, 4, 7, 8, 12, 16
food, 12
groups, 11
homes, 4, 7
sizes, 4, 16
sounds, 20
toes, 7
wings, 8, 15, 19